T0157115

Fulfilling Your God Given Destiny

THE MESSAGE TO THE BODY OF CHRIST

PRINCE E A JESHURUN

authorHOUSE®

AuthorHouse™
1663 Liberty Drive
Bloomington, IN 47403
www.authorhouse.com
Phone: 1-800-839-8640

All scripture quotations are taken from the King James Version, Amplified Version and new living translation version unless otherwise indicated.

Scripture quotations are taken from the King James Version (KJV) of the Bible—Public Domain.

Scripture quotations are taken from the Holy Bible, New Living Translation, copyright © 1996, 2004, 2007. Used by permission of Tyndale House Publishers, Inc., Carol Stream, Illinois 60188. All rights reserved.

Published by AuthorHouse   12/17/2012

ISBN: 978-1-4772-3428-0 (sc)
ISBN: 978-1-4772-3429-7 (e)

Library of Congress Control Number: 2012917772

Any people depicted in stock imagery provided by Thinkstock are models, and such images are being used for illustrative purposes only.
Certain stock imagery © Thinkstock.

This book is printed on acid-free paper.

This book is wholeheartedly dedicated to
Distinguished Senator **Ike Ikwerenmadu**,
the Deputy Senate President of the
Federal Republic of Nigeria.

CONTENTS

PREFACE

Do you know that, despite the widespread of church denominations around the world proclaiming the good news of our Lord Jesus Christ, a large number of believers are yet to grasp that reality of who they are made in Christ as New Creatures?

This profound statement may have aroused in your heart, an instant concern and attention of what could be responsible for the hindrances or delay of a Christian maturity in Christ.

Jesus Christ for the love of the father more than two thousand years ago, took upon Himself the death penalty that waited the children of the first Adam; paid with his blood, and judged sin on his cross and gave us a new kind of life superior to angels and Satan; what a blessing! He gave the manual called The Bible; that they discover in it all the blessing and work in its reality, through the power of the Holy Spirit. Therefore, the believer is a discoverer of divine realities in Christ helped by the Spirit to live the daily Christian life victoriously, expressing these realities.

The gospel of John 32; 8 declares 'and you shall know the truth and the truth shall make you free'. What truth is it? This is the truth of whom Christ has made you. Truth designed to affect your human spirit with the word of life. Beloved the Spirit desires that, the light of God's word show you how to perfect your faith in the body of Christ.

According to Ephesians chapter 4 verses 11-13,'And he gave some Apostles; and some, Prophets; and some Evangelists; and some, Pastors and Teachers; For the perfecting of the saints for the work of the ministry, for the edifying of the body of Christ: Till we all come in the unity of faith, and of the knowledge of the son of God, unto a perfect man, unto the measure of the stature of the fullness of Christ . . .'

Paul the Apostle ushers us into the knowledge of the purpose of ministry office, for the perfecting of the saints. Here perfecting refers to maturity. So that the saints be matured in the things of God that pertains ministry. For the work of the ministry, that saints all around world called the body of Christ do the work of the ministry, which is in two fold that is ministering to the world and ministering to the body of Christ. This is in the offering of service to the world and within the body of Christ.

To the world is the ministry of reconciliation, while the church is service to one another. Letting people in the world know that our heavenly Father is not counting on their wrongs as Jesus Christ has paid with his blood as a sacrificial lamb. Thirdly, for edification, to edify means to build, nurture etc. Therefore, they are fed with the knowledge of the person of Christ and the things that pertains His Kingdom.

The question is where does God's grace through His chosen servants affect a man in the New Testament dispensation? Is it his body, soul or spirit? Can a man as a soul comprehend the things of faith and leave a daily life of faith? Can he be able to have effective communication with God and heard? Is he to be guided by the law of The Spirit and faith, or by the Old Testament laws?

How can the believer distinguish himself where the spirit of the world is manifest?

The Word of God shows us expressly in the gospel of John chapter 3verse 5 declares 'except a man be born of water and of the Spirit, he cannot enter into the kingdom of God. That which is born of the flesh is flesh; and that which is born of the Spirit is spirit'. From this scripture, we realize that, it is the recreated human Spirit that gains acceptance into the kingdom not the flesh.

The Old Testament prophets were not born of the Spirit, but had the Spirit come upon them to accomplish a special assignment assigned of God. However, the New Testament believers were born of the Spirit, so had the Spirit guidance in their entire lifetime. This means the ministration is of the Spirit and affects the Spirit. Galatians chapter 3 verses five, 'Are ye so foolish? Having begun in the Spirit, are made perfect by the flesh?

Hebrews chapter 6 verse 1 declares 'Now faith is the substance of things hope for the evidence of things not seen'. If faith is, the evidence of things not seen and we know that the spiritual deals with all unseen realities, then both worked hand in hand. For faith deals with unseen realities same as the Spirit. Furthermore, it is not possible for a soul man to comprehend the things of faith because it is spiritually discern and communicated. In addition, the soul man cannot live what he cannot see spiritually as faith is the evidence of unseen realities, so is unable to communicate effectively with God. The believer in Christ should be guided by the law of the Spirit and faith, because it reciprocates the spiritual life given him. That which is of the flesh is flesh and that which is of the Spirit is Spirit; he absolutely has nothing to do with the Old Testament laws, knowing that he is born into a life of faith in Jesus the Christ.

The book of Acts records that it was the works of the early believers that made people call them Christians. They were seen do same things that Jesus deed.

Jesus made a remarkable statement as My Father worketh, so I work. What work?

The Father made all things in creation lastly made man in His Image and Likeness and said were all-good. Jesus came and did the same good work, healing the sick, raising the dead, delivering the oppressed and the sinner. Sickness, Oppression, disease and death are of the devil. Jesus with good works like the Father destroyed this works of the Devil.

Acts chapter 11 verse 19-26, 21 'the power of the Lord was with them, and a large number of this gentiles believed and turned to the Lord' '. . . When he arrived and saw this evidence of God's blessing, he was filled with joy, and he encouraged the believers to stay true to the Lord.'23.NLT.

It is clear that in a wicked world of ours, it is the good-works of a believer in the supply of the Spirit of Christ, which stands him out from the unbeliever. If the believers in Christ will replicate their master anywhere they find themselves in this present evil world in good works through his words, lifestyle and his hands, to send forth healing; without an iota of doubt his light will dominate the works of darkness; that *is a Christian* people will say.

Giving a believer a patterned way to leave The Christ life is not in agreement with New Testament teaching, because Jesus said that the Holy Spirit was responsible in guiding the believer into all truth, John chapter 16 verses 13. The believer by conscious study of the word, have the Word of God dominate his intellect to have the works of Christ manifested through him, to the benefit of his world. Then will people see the evidence of God's blessing as in Act of the Apostles.

Believers need in this end time to have Christ manifest in their human spirit, mind and body as it was with Paul in Galatians chapter 1 verse15-16 'But even before I was born, God chose me and called me by his marvelous grace. Then it pleased Him 16to reveal His son in me so that I would proclaim the Good News about Jesus to the Gentiles'.

Paul never allowed Peter's ministry over shadow his ministry. So he said, Peter's calling was to the Jews while his, to the Gentiles and even had to rebuke Peter when he erred avoiding the Gentiles that were not circumcised because of his Jewish friends.

Christ should through your good works, reveal to the unbelieving grace, to have an undefeated life here on earth.

You must understand that the connectivity that your human spirit has with God's Spirit helps you maintain and sustain the flow of communion with the Holy Spirit. Under this divine connectivity are we able to see our level in God and greater things of the SPIRIT, in a more Godly and friendly manner.

That is why taking bible school courses or graduating as a student of a Bible school, should not guarantee you into ministry office, because we minister to spirit beings with real spiritual need. It follows that, as ministers of the Spirit we go through spiritual training that will qualify us for a position in God, this truth is indispensable.

The law of the Spirit should always guide in our right stand with God as believers, because teachings that have bordered the five senses have been the major emphasis for decades in many denominations around the world. The Christian has been ordained into the spiritual life, in the guidance of the Word of God. The believer's life in Christ then is not, regulated by what he feels, thinks or sees, but by the Word and Spirit of God, which includes his manner of dressing, eating, speaking etc.

Galatians 5; 18 'But if ye be led off the Spirit, ye are not under the law'.

Galatians 5; 25 'If we live in the Spirit, let us also walk in the Spirit'.

In the believer resides the law of the Spirit that directs and guides him in the dos and don'ts of God. The first Epistle of John chapter 2 verse 27 tells us this, 'But the anointing which ye have received of Him abideth in you, and ye need not any man teach you: but as the same anointing teacheth you of all things, and is the truth, and is no lie, and even as it hath taught you, ye shall abide in Him'.

This anointing, the believer received the moment he made Jesus Christ the Lord of his life. This anointing guides and directs him in that path God ordained and planned for him before the foundation of the world.

Already in the believer is the guiding light of God residence, as he walks in the light of the Word, he goes in perfect guidance into his destiny.

So is out of order to make laws for a child of God to guide him/her, because something is wrong with the world's system in dressing, eating, and communication.

The Holy Spirit is the one responsible to showing the believer how not to conform or copy the behaviour and traditions of this world, as he is transformed into a new person in Christ by changing the way he thinks through the word. Romans chapter 12 verses 2.NLT.

The Holy Spirit, Jesus told us, will guide us into all truth. John chapter 16 verse 13. Some churches have made issues that affect the five senses a yardstick for being a citizen of God's kingdom. In addition, these same denominations through manmade doctrine have created some kind of barricade for the Spirit gaining mastery over the mind. Because doctrines that border the five senses only dominates the mind not the recreated human spirit. When that happens, it will only create a life style that is mental and sensual.

Prophet Ezekiel saw this reality as he spoke the mind of God in Chapter11 verses 19-20 'And I will give them one heart and I will put a new spirit within you ;and I will take the strong heart out of their flesh, and I will give them an heart of flesh;' after verse 19 has taken place verse 20, gives us the result 'That they may walk in my status, and keep my ordinances and do them; and they shall be my people, and I will be their God'.

One thing significant you should be keen to set your heart on is what it says in verse 19 *one heart and new spirit*, following verse 20 that they may walk in my statues . . .'

When you are born again, you posses that new spirit it talks about in your body vehicle. You are now a custodian of divine verities, God Spirit in you .What a blessing and privilege, to have God function through you.

Job had to say something about this, because he realized that it was God's Spirit in a man that made the difference. In chapter 32 of Job verse 8, 'But there is a spirit in man; and the inspiration of the Almighty giveth them understanding'.

Now from this word-based reality, we establish that, THE LAW OF THE SPIRIT is at work in one who believes and receives Christ as His Lord and Saviour.

God, has planned the believer's life before the foundation of the world, to rule in the affairs of life by the Spirit and word of God, and not by mental assent regulated by the five senses.

The Christian life is a daily victory over the flesh (the senses) in total yield to the Spirit of God.

Paul the Apostle in 1 Corinthians 15;31 declares, ' . . . I die daily'. Paul meant that in his daily life style of standing for the defence of the gospel, he puts away the deeds of the flesh to attain Christ.

The word of God shows more concern about the believers human spirit being adorn with the fruit of the recreated human spirit which is; meekness, gentleness, kindness, love etc and to the believer that should be his passion,1peter chapter3 verse3-4 reads 'don't be concerned about the outward beauty that depends on fancy hairstyles, expensive jewellery, or beautiful cloths. You should be known for the beauty that comes from within, the unfading beauty of a gentle and quiet spirit, which is precious to God' NLT Bible.

It is obvious that God is more concerned that the believer concentrates in nurturing his inner man, rather than the outer man, which has no significance in His presence, as it will perish. Importantly the believer must show moderation, and that means as Christ representative here on earth you must look good and presentable in all things, which exudes God's glory as light in the midst of a wicked and crocked world.

Even Christ our perfect example and master dressed in kingship apparel, that the roman soldiers desired his garment, and so parted it.

Of course, you know how attractive and beautiful kingship regalia is, that the Roman soldiers' took possession of His.

Paul pointed out from a higher spiritual level in Philippians chapter 1 verse 15, 16 and 17 'It's true that some are preaching out of jealousy and rivalry. But others preach Christ with pure motives . . . They preach with selfish ambition, not sincerely, intending to make my chains more painful to me'. Paul saw it differently, so preached from love viewpoint. He also asserts that other Ministers preached out of selfish ambition, some in pretence as in making his Chains painful in declaring the gospel message.

What chains? Chains of the gospel, in the proclamations of its truth. Let me make a point clearly understood in Galatians. Paul had same challenge with Galatians, saying who had cast an evil spell on him. For the meaning of Jesus Christ's was made as clear to you as if you had seen a picture of his death on the cross.

Let me ask you this one question: Did you receive the Holy Spirit by obeying the Law of Moses? Of course not! You received the Spirit because you believed the message you heard about Christ, Galatians chapter 3 verses 1-2. That is what it was like with Paul in his days, other ministers taught law and grace together as criteria of acceptance by God, which Paul in his gospel of love stood against.

The scenario that took place in Paul's day still re-occurs in our contemporary world and is responsible for the delay of the believer's maturity in Christ.

Grace and truth came from love in God. Love gives neither condition nor law to be kept or obeyed for a blessing. Grace means unmerited favour.

To the Jew, the law he could not keep was taken out of the way and nail to his cross; Colossians chapter 2 verses 14, KJV. To the Gentiles they were lost without God in the world, and are now called the children of God. What a blessing!

Now that you are in Christ, you have been made one with Him in the beloved.

Therefore, you realize that the man that has not received Christ, the solution is not that he confesses his sins. What do you want him to confess, when his whole life in the past has been encased in darkness? The man Jesus has settled every debt of sin, all he needs is believe and declare him as Lord and saviour of his life, and at the very Moment he does that, in him resides eternal life.

Finally, I know that this piece of work will inspire impact and motivate the individual believer and Clergy, to the realities of God's word, where the maturity of the believer in Christ resides.

Prince E A Jeshurun.

WHY THIS BOOK

'But even before I was born, God chose me and called me by his marvellous grace.

Then it pleased him to reveal his Son to me so that I would proclaim the good news about Jesus to the Gentiles. When this happened, I did not rush out to consult with any human being. Nor did I go up to Jerusalem to consult with those who were apostles before I was'. Galatians chapter 1 verse 15-17.

Glory is to God for raising men and women of God today who by the revelation of Jesus Christ made known the mind of God in Christ. With a greater light of the Word, they have brought clarity to subjects of doubt; this has inspired tremendous growth and increase in knowledge within the body of Christ.

I will make some point clear before I tell the why of this book.

Many people have defined revelation by their personal experiences. They could have had it in the dream, vision, or being translated, receiving an important message to be passed to another person or a group of people. All revelation has sources and come in various degrees.

Nevertheless, what I am going to share with you is revelation knowledge and it has nothing to do with dream, vision nor translation, but the WORD.

As a believer in Christ, you cannot experience the greater things of God if you are not hungry for Him. The greatest of all revelations is the revelation of the Word, and except you are hungry you cannot experience it. God still search for that man and woman he can show what to do to fix that missing link, causing His people wonder in darkness.

If the church can look inwards, and be, open to change by the word in the guidance Of the Spirit, there will be such a great manifestation of God's grace in our World.

The church has so much concentrated on sin than the WORD of GOD. However, Jesus dealt with the sin problem. The reason many have not understood this, is that some ministers of the gospel have not dwelt enough on the word, to see what they are supposed to see. Their minds have been with issues that cannot withstand the word. So, some are faced with partial spiritual blindness.

The only guide we have here on earth with us, is the Holy Spirit. He shows you how to go out and come in. If a church goes in circles know that she is out of the word.

It was a Wednesday service. I was sitting, in the second row, listening to the teaching of the word, when my spiritual eye was-opened to see the heart of one of the committed leader offering a partial service but with a fervent countenance.

In the midst of this spiritual drama, I suddenly saw that the virus of partial service had already spread to other leaders. There was such a convincing countenance of commitment and dedication without a revelation (an insight) of such commitment and dedication in the understanding of the word, and very unfortunate the pastor at that moment was not spiritual intone to know of this, because he was only concerned with an aspect of truth in the body of truth.

Sited bodily and my mind being influenced by the Holy Spirit to this truth, while the teaching in the Church was in progress, the Spirit of God told me write to the entire body of Christ, for same is depicted in most churches around the world. Again, He began to show me why certain past mishaps took place in the life of pastors in other denomination I knew, who were void of the revelation in the word (the living truth of God's word).

Christianity in the New Testament dispensation is completely different, because it speaks of life after the resurrection of Jesus Christ.

Some are serving the Jesus before resurrection and desire to be like Him. However, that Jesus was a sacrificial lamb. That is why you realize despite preaching consistently nothing miraculous takes place. Sometimes, you feel like going back to your secular job or private business as a minister. Are you still wondering, what I mean then? You are bound to struggle when you feel and think that your effort before God will give you credibility.

Perhaps you feel emptiness in your heart and think, is it Possible to partake in the rapture with other believers the moment the Master Jesus shows up as the scriptures assures. How will I partake in that event knowing I am born again as the Word assures me of seeing the kingdom of God? Well the answer is here relax and keep reading. Some even Preach faith, but see nothing of faith take place in their life, without a proof that the man Jesus truly died for them.

Understand this very moment that, the Jesus before resurrection and the Jesus after resurrection are not same. The Jesus of Nazareth that lived in Capernaum, as we have heard with twelve Disciples, was hungry, taught his disciples how to love their neighbour and enemy, is not known with the same knowledge after his resurrection, because they are two very different personalities.

Think about this for a moment, imagine you had a brother you slept in the same room, eat and play to gather. And on a particular day he is no more, after three days he surfaced and you suddenly see him going through the walls, not the door this time around and doesn't sleep in the house because he is here and there for Some very important assignment. Still continues his good works and finally tells you he is going back to where he came, and just ascends. Will you say you still know him?

'*Wherefore* henceforth know we no man after the flesh: yea though we have known Christ after the flesh, yet now henceforth know we him no more, 2 Corinthians chapter5 verses 16.

Therefore, if any man be in Christ, he is a new creature: old things are passed away; behold all things are become new'.

How do you know the resurrected Christ?

This comes to your human spirit by revelation knowledge in God's Word through the transportation of the Holy Spirit, Galatians chapter 1 verse 16.

What do I mean transportation of the Holy Spirit?

This is operational as the Holy Spirit through scriptures information, your hunger and passionate desire to know Christ and the power of His resurrection. The Holy Spirit, charges your human spirit to journey through events in the word from Old (the works of the word through the prophets) and New Testaments, pictures the word in your heart in the experience of His death, burial and resurrection and the new law that guide your life as a new creature in Christ.

It is unfortunate that some say the Holy Spirit ended with the Apostles in the day of Pentecost. I pray that God open the eye of understanding of such people, so that their lab our will not be in vain. How can the believer leave a victorious Christian life without the power of the Holy Spirit in this evil world? Of course, it is not possible. That is the reason Jesus told His disciples, 'and ye shall receive power, after that the Holy Spirit is come upon you . . . 'Act 1 verses 8. Without controversy, the Christian is only successful through the power of the Holy Spirit.

Every child of God, talks about the rapture of the church and wants to be rapture, but have not yet experienced the revelation of Jesus Christ in their human spirit. The revelation of Jesus in the believer is what must take place before the rapture. What a blessing to experience in glory!

This is the reason for this book that you walk in the light of God's word, to the believer in Christ, and the Clergyman.

The Believer

As a believer it matters who trains you morally and spiritually, because what you see and hear is what you become. Learn and be like the Berea Christians who will go searched the scripture diligently after they have received the Ministration of the word in the gathering of believers, if those things they heard were so, acts 17 verses 10 and 11. Whatever decision you make and stand upon in the Word, will sail you through whatever challenge. So be bold enough to take steps that will better you destiny in God.

Proverb 11 verses 9b declares 'but through knowledge shall the just (righteous) be delivered'.

The Minister

Be sure what you stand for; know what God has called you to do, Equip yourself not with Bible school knowledge alone, but with spiritual training under the school of the Holy Spirit, because you will only have a lifeless Church and lead people out of their destinies in God. You need a revealed body of knowledge in the Word. That means you must live a word study life guided in the inspiration of the Holy Spirit, which is your calling.

You are not a hireling, but called as a shepherd to lead this sheep to God's best for their lives.

Paul the Apostle made this remarkable statement in 1 Thessalonians chapter 2 verses 8, so affectionately longing for you, we were pleased to impart to you not only the gospel of God, but also our own life because you had become so dear to us.'

I am praying that your desire for the word and Spirit of God will guide you into the realities of your calling in Christ Jesus, in the spirit of revelation unto the day of our coming Lord and saviour. Amen.

INTRODUCTION

Through the inspiration of the Spirit the reasons for the unfulfilled life and ministry of the Christian was revealed to me, and how they can fulfil their God-given destiny with wisdom through the revelation of His Word.

I came to understand by the Spirit, that more that 90% of believers conscientiously serving in God's vineyard have no idea of their call in God. This was because of deficient spiritual insight into the plan and purposes of God in Christ. This has made many wonder into an unfulfilled life and ministry. In this same vein ministers of the gospel have made the flock move in a wrong route in their personal life. It is an issue of concern, but except the Spirit makes you see it.

It is pathetic that hundreds of thousands have been headed to the wrong vehicle in life which is the result of imperfect series of programmes (human traditions, ideologies, doctrines) encased in their minds (teachings that are not coherent with the revelation of God's word or mental assent). For this cause, an end must be brought, through the revelation of God's word, to this chaotic situation piloting the new creation into an unfulfilled life and ministry in Christ.

The gospel of our Lord Jesus Christ is indispensable, because it came not only to manifest the light of the kingdom in the midst of a wicked and crooked world but also to fulfil and perfect the believer's destiny in God, as the Spirit Word defines him.

The Lord said "get this truth announced, for there is so much I want those I have called my beloved to know in this very last moment, for only through knowledge shall they be put over from ignorance in what I have called and made them in Glory.

This knowledge enlightens you of the person of Christ Jesus in His exalted position in the heaven lies and inheritance He has handed to us as the heirs of the kingdom.

Ephesians 1 verses 17 and 18 declares, 'that the God of our Lord Jesus Christ the father of glory may give to you the spirit of wisdom and revelation in the knowledge of him; the eye of your understanding being enlightened; that you may know what is the hope of you calling and what are the riches of his glory of his inheritance in the saint, and what is the exceeding greatness of his Power . . .'

This was the prayer of Paul the apostle to the saint in Ephesus and still applies to believers today, that in the spirit of wisdom and revelation we live and walk in the knowledge of Christ. You have to be equipped with this truth to walk in Continues light in God.

CHAPTER ONE

DEFINED BY THE SPIRIT AND WORD

'And the earth was without form and void; and darkness was upon the face of the deed and the Spirit of God moved (hovered) upon the face of the water and God said let there be light and there was light and God saw that the light was good, and God divided the light from darkness,' Genesis chapter 1 verses 2.

It is obvious that in the beginning of the second creation that the earth was a chaotic mass, it would not have been in chaos if something did not happen to the first creation, so prophet Jeremiah in chapter 4 verses 23 to 26, from his words gives us a clear picture of the scenario that occurred that brought about the earth to chaos. He says in verse 26, that the earth was turned into wilderness because of God's fierce anger released on Lucifer. God because of His infinite love for creation decided to make the earth habitable by His Spirit.

The Holy Spirit was the first personality in the Godhead to show up on the scene, to redeem earth's glory. He alone had the capacity and infinite ability to restore the fallen state of the earth from God's viewpoint.

THE HOLY GHOST, the Bible says, hovered upon the face of the waters. What was He doing? Incubating, dominating and imparting His life into all earthly disfigured Creatures. The Holy Spirit was sanctifying the earth for God's blessing again, getting the earth ready for the seed of the Word. So in the same vain you realize without the Holy Spirit in the heart of a man the word cannot prosper.

What a wonder beholding the gracious work of the Spirit in its glory as it manifest, who without the earth maintains it deplorable state. Glory is to God.

Similarly, it is the convincing impact of the Holy Spirit upon the heart of the unregenerate man that makes him declare and receive in his heart the seed of the word, as he believes in Jesus as Lord and Saviour. Before this time, the spirit of the unsaved was without form and void and darkness upon it. How miserable is unsaved, for the seed of sin sown in his earthly father Adam through Lucifer is passed to his spirit. Because of this curse, have been separated from God.

We should give thanks to God almighty for sending His Holy Spirit to bless humanity. He convicts (John chapter 16 verses 8) the unsaved that he receives the seed of the word Jesus Christ, and is called the child of God, what a great placement!

The word of God declares that no man say that Jesus is Lord, but by the HOLY GHOST 1corinthians 12 verses 3b.

It is so important that we understand that, what God's Spirit have not incubated upon, He has no claims over it. The moment God by His Spirit has a graceful claim, and then is it completely and totally his. Through the impact and influence of the Spirit and the Word in a believer, he is defined and figured out as God's possession.

The believer has a new identity, through his definition. His definition says, He is a child of God, a brother of Jesus Christ, a citizen of God's kingdom, is that not lovely being identified as God's possession, sure it is. Hallelujah.

The moment the word of God is declared in power, it brings fought, that we may behold the works and believe in our hearts, and extends that touch to others. To fulfil your God given destiny is being defined by the Spirit and Word of God. Did you say how? Common that still small voice is saying right in your heart speaking to you about victory over the world, convincing you to declare that Jesus Christ is Lord of your life. That is the voice of the Holy Spirit, He wants you to belong to God's big, family and be his child. Say yes to Him and begin this glorious life in Christ.

I know you believe he died for you, because he loved you and wants you the best.

The Word in the Mind

Man is a spirit; he has a soul and lives in a body. When you are defined by God' Spirit and Word, meaning you are born again, your life style must be in Conformity with the Word of God. It is your human spirit that is born again not your mind.

The will of your mind desires to continue in that worldly flow, so will fight to Influence your body and intellect in that former life style, but you will discover how to bring it under word control in the word.

When God's Spirit and Word defines a man, John 3verses 5. He is saved not his soul. The soul (mind) is the seat of desire, motive and action. The mind is transformed when the word of God gains mastery over it. The mind needs be educated, reprogrammed out of the world systems to the structures of God's word.

And be not conformed to this world(age) but be ye transformed (TRANSFIGURED) by the renewing of your mind, that ye may prove what is good, and acceptable, and perfect, will of God, Romans 12 verses 2.

Let me give you an instance with a cassette. A cassette recorded with a music that is out of fashion, happens to be in your possession, as you still need that cassette for some very important purpose and assignment. The purpose is to record a Christian message that will bless people's lives. What will you do then?

It is to simply delete the old music and record the new message. This is what happens when you are born again. God dislikes that old life style, and He wants to get rid of that character, through His word and have His word rule your life.

'Now ye are clean through the word which I have spoken to you' John 15 verses 3. Change your mind with God's word.

Why the Transformation of your Mind is Important

God's plans and purpose for your life is to express His glory here on earth. Jesus showed us as he healed a blind boy who the Pharisee asked how he came about his sight. Jesus was asked, if it was the sin of the parent that made the boy blind, but He answered that the works (glory) of God be manifest.

'This beginning of miracles did Jesus in Cana of Galilee, and manifested forth his glory; and his disciples believed in him' John chapter 2 verses 11. The moment your life turns a blessing to another it means the glory of God is manifest through you.

As believers, our human spirit is structured to relate with God, Who is a Spirit. Moreover, our mind relates with physical things here on earth with human beings. To make manifest the spiritual kingdom and impart humanity with the blessings in this kingdom, our minds must be controlled in the word of God.

Therefore, it follows that your impact here on earth is greatly dependent on how affected your mind is by God's word. Meaning, a greater dimension of the word in your mind, the greater the manifestation of God's glory through you in your world.

This is the reason after you are born of the Spirit; you have to start working on the transformation of your mind, to conform to the will and mind of the Father. To think what He thinks, say what He says, and love what He loves. That is the perfect work of His Word as you yield to His voice.

Never let your life be intimidated or limited by the state of your mind, as you see through the lens of faith in God's perspective in His Word, because there are greater things you have been ordained to achieve and enjoy.

The Word answer

The Word of God is an album containing the images of your success, victory, prosperity, healing, miracle, inheritance, as constantly behold it reveals your identity.

'But we all, with open face beholding as in a glass(word) the glory of the Lord are changed into the same image from glory to glory, even by the Spirit of the Lord'.

The Spirit, through the word, constantly reveals the true picture of the believer as he set a constant gaze on the glory (works of grace) of the Lord. Under the transforming euphoria of His word seizes to be held back introspectively, for Christ reveals Himself through him.

What a blessed life that, the chaos hindering your increase and expansion now is, transplanted with the blessing of increase and expansion.

'To Whom God would make known what is the riches of the glory of the mystery among the Gentiles, which is Christ in you the hope of glory', Colossians 1verses 27.

God's word is quick and powerful than any to double-edge sword; it pierces the soul and excavates false pictures in your mind Hebrews 4 verses 12.

The word permeates, and sustains impact upon the human mind making it Gods home.

God's word alone conveys the new creations picture, identity, integrity, and destiny and possess the transformative potency. 'And have put on the new man who is renewed in knowledge after the image of Him that created Him', Colossians 3 verses 10.

Many years back in ignorance, I came to believe some folks who said that what a man will become in this life is absolutely dependant on being industrious and academic qualification.

Nevertheless, my mentality was altered by the word as I soon discovered that 'the fastest runner doesn't always win the race, and the strongest warrior doesn't always win the battle, the wise some sometimes go hungry and the skilful are not necessarily wealthy. In addition, those educated do not always lead successful lives. It is all decided by chance, by being in the right place at the right time. Ecclesiastic chapter 9 verse 11. 'Promotion does not come from the north, south east, west, but cometh from the Lord'. psalm 75 verses 6.

Life consists of the deposit of God's treasure in your heart, which is His word. Get this right, I am not saying that education is irrelevant. It is relevant, but do not be influenced by it, for certificate gets you a job. True Knowledge is gotten in the word of God.

Life answers not to struggles and much suffering, life answers to principles of God's word. You need to inundate your spirit, soul and body with the life of the Word of God as you declares what He says concerning you.

Let Christ dwell in you richly in all wisdom, teaching and admonishing one another in psalm and hymns and spiritual songs, singing with grace in your hearts to The Lord' Colossians 3 verses 16.

The Human Spirit: The Real Man

Earlier on, I said that man is a spirit; he has a soul and dwells in a body. The spirit man is the real man. Who a man is, is the function of his spirit. And his Spirit is God's contact point. Therefore, John in his gospel said except a man is born of the Spirit and the Word he cannot see the kingdom of God. So this means as you are born of the spirit, you gain a spiritual insight and entrance into the Kingdom.

"Verily verily I say unto you except a man be born again, he cannot see the kingdom of God, Nicodemus saith unto him, can a man be born again when he is old? Jesus answered, verily I say unto thee, except a man be born of water and of the spirit, he cannot enter into the kingdom of God."

The issue of concern is directly from the words of Jesus, except a man be born of the Spirit he cannot see, He further stressed what is of the flesh is flesh and spirit is spirit.

Therefore, we concur that the Spirit recreates the human spirit, meaning the spirit is the real man.

To make this point further clear, the necessity for the need to be born again was as the result of the fall of Adam in disobedience. That made all humankind from Adam loose connectivity with God's Spirit.

However, for God's love for humankind sent His only begotten son full of grace and truth to restore humanity back to the Father. This makes being born of the Spirit a necessary requirement into the kingdom.

Beloved in Christ the generation of natural men is passed forever, this are the days where spirit beings in Christ rule in the affairs of this life recognized in heaven, earth and the earth beneath. In these last days, you will realize a great number of death of humans but 0% for the new creature in Christ.

Jesus Christ put an end to the Adamic race and commenced a new race, called the new creatures (spirit beings). Be awakened to this reality and be conscious that the recreated human spirit is who you really are.

Function With the Spirit Law

'As many that believe in His name, to them gave He power to become the sons of God.'

Gospel of John chapter 1 verses 12.

The believer in Christ is not guided by physical law; he functions not with the physical life. He is not led by the dictate of the senses, as he is a spirit being.

"For they that are after the flesh do mind the things of the flesh; but they that are after the Spirit the things of the Spirit. For to be carnally minded is death; but to be spiritually minded is life and peace, because the carnal mind is enmity towards God. For it is not subject to the law of God neither indeed can be" Romans 8: verses 5 and 7

The question is what is the law of the Spirit? Remember John 4 verses 24 "God is a Spirit, and they that worship him must worship Him in spirit and in truth" This means God's law is spiritual, because He the Spirit, you walk in the spirit to gain His attention. Therefore, your entire life as a believer in the offering of service is bound to the spiritual laws (spiritual life).

CHAPTER TWO

DEFINED BY THE SPIRIT AND WORD

The ministry of the Spirit and Word of God is the anchor pilot of the Christian destiny in the offering of service in the body of Christ.

This is clear in Genesis chapter 1 verse 2, how the writer through the inspiration of the Holy Spirit in the book pictures the unprecedented act of the person of the Holy Spirit brooding over the surface of the waters. In that influence, imparting life into everything turned chaos, because of judgment by God.

The Holy Spirit the author of life from the very beginning was the actor in the restoration of the creation. He has spoken through the mouth of the prophets, guided, inspired and moved them in the path of their calling in God. He also confirms their declarations as servants of Jehovah.

Big brother John in his gospel chapter 1verse1 declares, 'in the beginning was the word and the Word was with God and the word was God'. What a statement of life.

The word of God in the beginning of creation was resident in the Father and was not revealed as Jesus. The word came into play of creativity as the Holy Spirit having had entire dominance on the chaotic creation, giving all a branded definition-in that act restoring the Fathers creation.

Marvelous it is in our sight to gain insight into the mighty and gracious work of the Spirit. In that euphoria we appreciate to appropriate those truth meant for us to enjoy as kingdom citizens.

As it was in the beginning the Spirit and Word of God made manifest creation and the Spirit and the Word recreates a man in the New Testament, it follows also that The Spirit and Word defines the believer's destiny, plan and purpose in God and matures him, son.

Life with the Spirit and Word of God is full of dynamism, beauty and glory. For this cause do not allow anything deter you of that glory or make you less than He has planned for you as His beloved.

Attaining Maturity in Christ

In God is neither weakness nor incompleteness, 'for in Him we are complete', Colossians chapter 2 verse 19.

The Word says the believer is His representative here on earth, 2corinthians 5 19-20, which means in the believer God has invested all His greatness through Christ, to act on His behalf. Imagine what result you will command as God's number one man.

When a child is born into planet earth, he is a human person. Before that time, still in the womb of his mother, he was yet to be called somebody. Now he has an identity. He has hands, legs, mouth eye, ear, nostril etc. This is same experience with a born again child of God.

To become a matured man or woman, you must under parental tutorship learn culture, Custom and how to go through the affairs of life and turn a success.

Maturity here again gains him another identity as a complete and matured man. This experience is not different from the Christian experience, same as when one is born again; he gains an identity as a child in the kingdom. As he attains maturity in living in instructions from authority above him, he gains another identity as the Spirit and the Word of God define him.

Chapter one of this book talked about being defined by the Spirit and the word, this is the born again stage. Chapter two also talks about being defined by the Spirit and the Word of God, which deals with the maturity stage.

The believer in Christ is given double recognition from the moment he gave his life to Christ and as he attains his maturity in Christ. This is very important to understand and take note, because we see this same thing in the life of Jesus Christ. From when He was baptized to when He was through fasting forty days and night, the Father in the midst of people and his disciples made two different statements.

Before we get to the in-depth of these realities I will bring to light what the believer is to work with to attain maturity in Christ.

In Christendom today, there are many children of God and very few matured sons of God and it is an issue of serious concern to the body of Christ. Moreover, the reason for this, is not Far-fetched, the teaching of law and grace as the word of God for the New Testament believer.

Laws and manmade doctrine that border the five senses they teach to guide the baby believer from worldliness so will not be distract acted, and avoid affecting his faith. When I say law I mean the old Testament commandment, thou shall not, and thou shall not. These laws were physical laws to be obeyed by children of Israel for a blessing. However, in the New Testament the giver of that law leaves in us. Therefore, we are to listen to His voice and do what He tells us. We don't need to look at an outward written law to obey it. The New Testament believer has been fashioned to do the word and not to obey. There are two walls of difference between just going ahead to do something because it is that nature in a person to do it, to just giving an instruction to be obeyed. Let us consider man made doctrines. These are teachings that border the five senses. Man made doctrine always yearn to set a physical pattern that tries to show spiritual sense, rather than allowing The Spirit to guide in such decisions. Let us see what law is up to.

Man made doctrine and extraction of laws from the Old Testament taught as grace from God, will never mature the believer in Christ. This is clear in the word of God. The Bible says you must live in full compliance of the law, if you want to live by the law. That is not possible because is grace that worketh in us. 'For when I tried to keep the law, it condemned me. So I died to the law that-I stopped trying to meet the requirements-so that I might live for God', Galatians 2 verse 19 NLT. ' . . . For no one will ever be right with God by obeying the law' 2 verse 16b.

'But those who depend on the law to make them right with God are under curse, for the scripture say, Curse is everyone who does not observe and obey all the commands that are written in God's book of the law'. Therefore, it is clear that no one can be made right with God by trying to keep the law. For the scripture say, 'it is through faith that a righteous person has life' Galatians 3 verses 10-11.

Paul further spoke to the Jews because it was to them the law was given in Galatians chapter 4 verses 1, 'Think of it this way. If a father dies and leaves an inheritance for his young children, those children are not much better off than slaves until they grow up, even though they actually own everything their Father had.

They have to obey their guardians until they reach whatever age their father set.

Moreover, that is the way it was with us before Christ came. We were like children; we were slaves to the basic spiritual principles of this world. 4 But when the right time came, God sent His Son, born of a woman, subject to the law.

5 God sent Him to buy freedom for us who were slaves to the law; so that he could adopt us as his very own children. The next verse is very

power full, 6 And because we are his children, God has sent the Spirit of his son into our hearts, prompting us to call out, 'Abba Father' Galatians chapter 4 verses 1-6.NLT.

The above scripture has made it clear that as a believer in Christ you have no business with the law rather the faith life in Christ. The law as a school master mentored in the absence of the messiah, but when messiah came (the owner of the house) Mr Law business came to end, so that messiah can now do the family business with family members.

Manmade doctrine borders the five senses. It tries to control externals, which includes what you see, touch, feel, taste etc. It is important to understand that the Christian life is not controlled nor regulated by externals, because 2 Corinthians' 4verse 18 says 'while we look not at the things, which are seen: for the things that are seen are temporal; but the things, which are not seen, are eternal'. All that revolves the five senses are things that are seen, they do not possess eternal value. So that we walk by faith not by sight (sensory perception)

Since, we have realized from the word that the law and manmade doctrine bordering the five senses do not mature a believer in Christ but faith in Christ.

Hence, the life of the believer is absolute faith in the word, as the righteous shall live by faith in all undertakings. The Law of the Spirit and Word becomes the believer's new law. Glory is to God!

The testimony of the Holy Spirit about Jesus Christ is what the believer lives by.

A New Definition

When you come to the Father through Jesus Christ as a child, He wants you to grow to maturity. You start in desiring the sincere milk of the word as a babe, 1peter 2 verses 2. In baby level stage the Father relates to you as a baby, whatever that is profitable to your growth that you ask Him he will give you. It is important that you note that your growth is determined by your desire and hunger for the milk of the word. So the more you desire the more you grow, you will realize this sudden desire you develop that makes you enjoy studying the word and praying, that is the hunger! Being a babe, you are expected to know or be taught the elementary things that pertains your faith in Christ, until you attain your next level of growth, Hebrews 6 verses 1 and 2.

Now who indicates in your human spirit that you have moved to a new level?

Of course, it is the Holy Spirit. It comes a time that you suddenly realize loss of interest in those elementary teachings to strong meat of the word. This are hard truth. The point here is this, being born again makes you possess a definition in your human spirit as a child.

This definition of you, says you are a child of God, born of God, have eternal life in your spirit, you are seated with Christ Jesus in the heavenly realm, you are superior to the devil and angels. Come on brothers and sisters in Christ, what a marvellous blessing we have been granted as children in Christ.

There is yet another definition here, all creation listens to you without objection. That is what this chapter seeks to expound. How are you to attain that level? This is very important; do not miss out of this life transforming realities in this chapter.

This definition is the work of the Spirit as He guides you through the Word of God into the deep things of the Father, showing you how you relate and handle them.

This process as the Spirit guides you conveys in it, a definitive transforming power, that continually proceeds a new you, meaning a new definition of your Perspective. I mean something leaves your mind and spirit as the new personality (Christ), takes his abode in you. Proverbs 25 verse 4 'take away the dross from the silver, and there shall come forth a vessel for the finer'. This you will feel within you. Have you observed this with snakes, that after some time the old skin goes off as a new one is replaced. It same thing as the Holy Spirit takes off layers of your worldly mindset replaced with His nature and character.

You're Assignment

As you receive instructions from the word and perform assignments of the Spirit with that expected result, you are brought in and introduced into a new level platform to function for the purpose of kingdom business.

This gives you a definition, and creates awareness amongst the cloud of witnesses in the presence of God.

The definitive work is continues impact of the Spirit upon your human spirit, until you achieve the measure, statue and fullness of Christ unto a perfect man.

Yielding and walking in the light of the Word of God continually gives you a place in God's kingdom. You are presented before the cloud of witnesses as one of those sons `of God, who has through the power of the Spirit and the word, control the element of this present world. No one can have a place in the kingdom except the Spirit and Word define him.

It is mandatory as a believer, that you get your needs supplied within the confines of God's word. This truth was evident in the statement of Paul the Apostle when he said, 'Fight the good fight of faith' 1 Timothy 6 verses 12. He is telling you through the word of God by faith eye, lay hold on the unseen realities God has given you through Christ, through the confessions of the word. These realities can slip from your heart that is why he says you should lay hold on it. This is the reason I feel sorry for some children of God who are yet to possess the good things of this life by faith in the word because they will lose them. It is only the word, which can give without taking back.

'Thy word is a lamp unto my feet and a light unto my path' psalm 119 verses 105.

As a son under training, you must move with the lamp of the word. What does the word as a lamp do? It brings to your notice how to go about your immediate affairs and as a light informs you about the future.

You can't go out to perform any business you are engaged and turn out a success, if the word doesn't guide your feet and path. Do you remember, what Lucifer told Jesus, (jump from the pinnacle and God will send His angels on your behalf so that you will not dash your feet). He meant Jesus should just go about his own things and God will protect Him.

However, you see Jesus was only concerned with the will of His Father.

The devil does that today, he tells someone live anyhow and God will protect you.

For your information, God only protects His word that it happens. So aligning yourself with the word of God gives you a sure guarantee, of your success.

There are troubles in this life, we must as sons through the wisdom of the word in us overcome whatever challenge it offers. The word of God says that you have overcome the world, because greater is He that is in you than He, that is in the world,1John chapter 4 verses 4. It does not matter, how great the mountain looks, it has already been overcome. Hallelujah.

Commitment and Dedication

You must attain son ship by commitment and dedication in your local assembly.

You must be entirely devoted and consumed in the passion of that Godly business in your charge and be trusted, with regular feedbacks.

Instructions must be taken and Performed from the one in place of authority, because in the body of Christ we are called to serve and walk in authority. In addition, the way we respond regularly to our call for Service determines who we are in His presence.

The Holy Spirit through our sincere yield in service defines us. I said this definitive process is transformative, it conforms us to the image of Christ.

Jesus Christ was in the business of doing just as He saw the Father did during creation, making things good. Never a time did Jesus left the Father's will for His.

A New Identity

'And Jesus, when he was baptized, went up straightway out of the water: and, lo, the heavens were opened unto him, and he saw the Spirit of God descending like a dove, and lighting upon him: And lo a voice from heaven, saying, this is my beloved Son, in whom I am well pleased', Matthew 3 verses 16 and 17, KJV.

While he thus spake, there came a cloud, and overshadowed them: and they feared as they entered into the cloud.

And there came a voice out of the cloud, saying, This is my beloved son: hear him. Luke 9 verses 34-35.

Here are to two thought provoking and powerful statement made by the FATHER Himself. However, the later more powerful than the former because it is the conferment of authorities to rule, dominate, permeate and control in heaven, earth and beneath the earth.

All power in heaven, earth and beneath the earth belongs to Him, the Father, before Jesus showed up as the son of man.

God the Father did not confer the authority to control the spiritual and physical world to Jesus at baptism. why? In baptism the Father said "He was pleased with Him", but in transfiguration He said "hear Him". After the baptism of Jesus, He moved into the wilderness to be tempted of the devil. At baptism, He did not have under control the spiritual and physical element, so the Father said He was pleased with Him. The story changed after Jesus had made a mess of the works of darkness, {demon possession, disease, sin, etc}, brought under absolute control living and non-living things. Then did the Father confer the authority in heaven, earth and the earth beneath to Jesus.

Now full of the Holy Ghost and power, He brought to control through the power of the Spirit and the words of the prophet the spiritual and physical world.

This He kept at, until a day came when He took his disciples for a prayer outing and the glory of God was manifest in the presence of His disciples, the Father made a statement different from the day of his baptism, This is my beloved Son: hear him.

The Father spoke to all creation, saying henceforth never you ask me for anything again children of Adam and eve, see my first born he has all the answers, He will Give you, angels listen to my first born, Satan listen to my first born, but there is nothing for you, living and non-living things listen to Jesus.

That is the reason nobody can come to the Father except through Jesus our Lord, Master and saviour, John chapter 6 verses 6.

Now that you have come to the Father through Him (Jesus), the Father also desires that every of His child attain son ship like Jesus. Therefore, as we prove our son ship eventually the Father will also declare listen to him/her, Glory to God.

I believe in you, I believe in your future in Christ, because I know you are getting there.

Declarations

The present world system that challenges you sonship can never have affect you, because big brother Jesus had already conquered them. Your love has prevailed, His life is at work in you, you are an over comer. The day you were born again, you were initiated into the cult of Jesus Christ and so you belong to Him. Hallelujah

The Holy Spirit and the Word of God only gives us the only acceptable definition that God requires to qualify us for the best things of God. The Spirit and Word of God brought creation into existence and will sustain for eternity creation.

In my final words in this chapter, I will want to stress that, spiritual maturity is that ability to understand and handle the things of God in the kingdom, with the spiritual sense in accordance with the Word concerning every issue and perspective of life in the idea of God's plan and purposes in Christ.

CHAPTER THREE
WALKING THE WORD TO BECOME
THE LIVING WORD

The Bible in the Gospel of John chapter 1 verses 1-3 declares, "in the beginning was the word and the word was with God and word was God. The same was in the beginning with God. All things were made by Him, and without Him was not anything made that was made".

As a believer in Christ, You have to come to understand from the testimony of the word that everything existing in heaven, earth and beneath the earth is a product of the Word, including all unseen creation. With this word-based information we concur that both the physical and spiritual world are product of the Word, and the word is the source of all existence. Knowing that the word is the source of all creations, it follows that the word sustains their existence.

The word of God has creative ability to perform anything declared to achieve with definite and specific result. The word was that dynamic ability the prophets of old possessed in their heart that kept them inspired, as they remained committed to their assignment given by God. These great men of God exercised themselves in moving with the light of God's word as instructed by God. Father Abraham was made the Father of many nations as he walked in the light of God's word; Noah walked in the light of the word and built the ark of redemption, Moses followed the same foot step as by the word brought deliverance to the children of Israel.

"This book of the law shall not depart from thy mouth; but thou shall meditate therein day and night, that thou mayest observe to do according to all that is written therein: for then thou shall make thy way prosperous, and then thou shall have good success" Joshua I verses 8.

Do you see that even the Old Testament prophets had success, victory in battle because they passionately walked in the light of the word? Joshua conquered nations as he walked in the light of God's word. This means victory was never with weapons of war for the children of Israel unlike their enemies that did trust on physical weapons.

Revelation chapter 19 verses 13 make it obvious that Jesus is the word, ' . . . and his name is called the WORD of GOD'.

In the New Testament church, we are graced walking in the light of God's word to Old Testament believers, because we are recreated spirit. Moreover, the Holy Spirit indwells us, unlike the Old Testament that the Spirit comes upon them for a special assignment, which was temporal. What a privilege granted us to enjoy!

Walking in the word to become the word is living under the word, in the word, through the word and above the word. This is a present hour reality as you become skilful in handling the word of righteousness through the power of the HOLY SPIRIT. Becoming the word is that your life expresses those good works the word displays, just like with the Father in creation in making things good through his very words of creation and in Jesus days as he healed and delivered the oppressed stepping into the word through the power of the Spirit, Luke chapter 4 verses 18-21.

Now that you are in Christ, your source and sustainer is the word, no more any less. Your life is become word based. The human life has been transplanted with the Spirit life. 'Who owes their birth neither to blood nor the will of the flesh (the physical) nor to the will of man (of a natural father), but of God' John chapter 1 verses 13 AMP.

'And this is that testimony (that evidence), God gave us eternal life, and this life is in His son. He who possesses the son of God has that life. He who does not possess the son does not have that life', 1 John 5 verses 11-12 Amp.

I brought these scriptures to your attention that I might establish the fact that your source determines your means and end. The self same word of God that you believed and confessed is same to govern your entire life endeavours. The above scriptures are the sayings of the word; somebody cannot just do what he feels to be accepted by God because they are good works. Actions must be inspired by the word for works to be accepted by the Father.

The believer works in the word as He takes every step in the direction and guidance of the Word. Put to work every word you hear from God's servant in your local assembly. Be crazy-ready to hear, receive and act on God's word. Before you get to the crazy level, start responding and making use of the word wherever you hear it, you are charting you course into being engulfed in the word. Praise God.

In the light of Revelation Knowledge

The Revelation of Jesus Christ in our human spirit through the power of the Spirit is becoming the much spoken word. I explained above that, the Jesus before resurrection is not the same Jesus after resurrection. Both have physical and spiritual knowledge.

The Jesus before resurrection is recognized by physical knowledge, which deals with what you see, while the Holy Spirit dealing with what you do not see knows the Jesus after resurrection, with spiritual knowledge. If you are hungry and desire to walk in the revelation knowledge of Jesus Christ, it becomes easy.

Secondly, do you have the infilling of the Holy Spirit? This is very important because it is all about spiritual knowledge, and it takes the Spirit to receive this knowledge.

This man Jesus after His resurrection is a spiritual man and it takes a spiritual man to receive His spiritual blessing. So what? Understand this truth, position your mindset through this information that is coming to you, and receive. It is yours hallelujah.

Personal Study

I believe that you have in your human spirit a burning desire to walk in the word to become the word.

'This book of the law shall not depart out of thy mouth, but thou shall meditate therein day and night, that thou mayest observe to do according to all that is written therein: for then thou shall make thy way prosperous, and have good success' Joshua 1 verses 8.

To study involves two things, reading and meditating. Reading is saying aloud, word to word what is written in the word concerning you; while meditation from the Greek word denotes mutter, which is to contemplate over those words you read and say under your breath continually until that effect is felt in your heart in conformity to your confessions. The study life must be a daily life style, aimed at being transformed in conformity to the image of Christ who recreated u, 'For God knew His people in advance, and he chose them to become like His son, so that His son will be the first born among many brothers and sisters' Romans 8 verses 29.

' . . . Instead, let the Spirit renew your thought and attitudes. 24 put on your new nature, created to be like God-truly righteous and holy', Ephesians 4 verses 23.

Engaging in spiritual exercises to build your spiritual muscles, it is what gives you the stamina and establishment in God. That is the reason you must take serious your study life because it is what ushers you into the revelation knowledge of Jesus Christ. By the words you meditate, you are constantly inspired walking in the will of the Father in the entirety of your life.

Some people think and do say that the word is settled for just certain aspect of their lives, but that is the lie of the devil. The psalms realized that one who put his trust in Jehovah needs the light of the word to go through this dark and confused world so said, "Thy word is a lamp unto my feet and light to my path." Think about this for a moment, you need your feet take you anywhere and everywhere you desire to go. If this is a fact, then where on this earth that your feet only conveys certain aspect of your body, not in totality. We need to see to understand whatever enterprise we get ourselves involved to better know how best to go about it. Moreover, the word is that lamp and light that helps us see into the dark (hidden plans and agenda of earthly men), hence the reason we must walk in the light of His word.

Transportation by Confessions

You became a member of the body of Christ through the very words of your mouth confessing Him Lord and Saviour of your life. Romans chapter 10 verses 7-10.

In that same manner, the very words of your mouth will determine your transportation into God's destiny for your life. In addition, the process of becoming the word, the word of God transports you as you with your mouth justify yourself. Is important you know that in the things of God without action, everything remains in it permanent place of rest, until the force of words through the power of the Spirit come to play. 'We having the same spirit of faith, according as it is written, I believe, and therefore have we spoken; we also believe, and therefore speak'. Speak it until you get there, and continue speaking even after getting there.2 Corinthians 4 verse 13.

Transportation I believe you know is the movement or conveyance of someone goods from one place to another. Transportation is also the conveyance of words from one person to the other. A word is also something that performs when spoken, as an instruction to another person. You cannot say, the words you speak on a daily bases as a child of God is nothing or makes no impact even if you do not see an instant result. Your words make instant spiritual change, but cannot be seen physically. Nevertheless, with time it will be manifested physically. Saying so, means we are daily living an empty life. Again it could be true in a negative sense if the person in question has sin nature. If you are a child of God, your words are pregnant with great possibilities, to change a life.

Thank God, we are all important personalities to God almighty. As we declare, confess our inheritance, victory, and success the word has established for our enjoyment, God through the power of the Holy Spirit makes it so. In other words, the Holy Spirit transport and moves the very word of God we confess into eternity in God, and transport our answers to us. ' . . . For He hath said, I will never leave thee, nor forsake thee. So that we may boldly say, The Lord is my helper, and I will not fear what man shall do unto me', Hebrews 13 verses 5b-6.

Do you realize that God had already said what you will become, more than a conqueror Romans 8 verses 37. What are you to do now, since you have known what your Heavenly Father has said concerning you? Hey! It is simple say the same thing that is what Paul meant in Hebrews.

The Greek word for confession is Homologia, meaning saying the same thing in consent. Therefore, confession in this sense demands that you say the same with God, as you are now one in Him. Saying the same thing in the manner God says it, makes you identify yourself with Him and that makes you inseparable from Him. This is a great privilege and blessing we enjoy in Christ. I now understand why Jesus told His disciples that many prophets have desired to see His day, and were not privileged. In Jesus day as you declare the word, you instantly become what it says. However, here are they privileged as mere disciples enjoying and sharing in His glory.

It is the same with the believer today sharing in His beauty and glory. Thanks and glory be to God our Father who has in these last days brought us into the beloved.

Make your confession a life style, your becoming the very word is embedded in it. Be transported by your confessions.

Act the Word

I really feel sorry for some believers who still believe that doing some acrobatic display shouting, jumping, running when praying and further asking God to send down fire from heaven, in the manner of prophet Elijah's manifestation in the destroying the prophets of Baal, to gets God's attention about a particular situation.

Elijah's day, is not the same with Jesus Christ day. James and John were prepared to call down fire from heaven, but Jesus was against their act by saying that he came to save not to destroy,' Luke chapter 9 verse 54. Let's find out what happed during the Transfiguration. Verses 30 of Luke chapter 9, declares 'that Elijah and Moses appeared on the mount with Jesus and were transfigured, but the Father hear Jesus; not Moses nor Elijah. Then why do you want to celebrate shadows while reality is with you. Today you hear some believers saying my Lord will do it for me. They keep saying that out of blind pride and nothing to show forth the empty talk.

Beloved to change things or get God's word working for you, you have to find out what it says about the situation that fights your faith, and just act what it says.

Jesus showed us how this works, as He, in the gospel of Luke chapter 4 verses 18 and21, steps into the word and fulfilled it in the eye of many witnesses.

The present hour Need

The present hour need is what places a demand on the word and through power of the Holy Spirit needs an immediate response. Jesus saw need in His immediate world, the lame, and blind, diseased in body, poor and sinner needed good news that will change their life story. Moreover, the power to get this done was embedded in the anointing of the Holy Spirit. Jesus recognized this truth, and so made His announcement that every one hears what the word has to say about Him. The moment He was through with His announcement seeks for an opportunity to affirm his words, casting out an unclean spirit from a man.

This principle is same today; you can truly have whatever you need to make your life great. Announce the word of God to your situation because they have ears and will hear you. Do you remember that Moses stroke the rock as was commanded of the Lord and water come out of it. Meaning the rock had ears to hear and did respond. There is no situation that will not respond to God's word from your mouth, they are bound to, for at the mention of the name of Jesus every knee must bow and every tongue confess that Jesus is Lord to the Glory of God the Father.

The very moment you declare the word to that situation and do act your confession you will definitely see a miracle. Stop being among those groups who wait for something to come or fall down from heaven before they believe the gospel; it will never happen, because that is not in agreement with the word. The word says believe and speak, and you have result to the Glory of God the father.

'Now unto Him that is able to do exceedingly abundantly and above that we ask or think, according to the power that worketh in us', Ephesians 3 verses 20.

'Ye ask and receive not, because ye ask amiss, that ye may consume it upon your lust', James 4 verses 3. The Christian life is a life of working on the waters, just like peter was called to walk on water. You have been called to work out the word of God to every situation of life's challenges. Act the word today.

CHAPTER FOUR

TREASURE IN THE HOUSE

The principle of the words

'A good man out of the good treasure of his heart bringeth forth good things: and an evil man out of the evil treasure bringeth forth evil thing', Matthew chapter 12 verses 35.

'Again the kingdom of heaven is like unto treasure hid in a field; the which when a man hath found, he hideth, and for joy thereof goeth and selleth all that he hath, and buyeth that field,' Mathew chapter 13 verses 44.

Treasure according Encarta English dictionary, is something of great value or worth.

The first scripture above declares 'a good man out of the good treasures of his heart bringeth forth good things'. Important to ask is, what kind of treasure is found in the heart? The answer is still found in the scriptures, ' . . . for out of the abundance of the heart the mouth speaketh'? Matthew chapter 12 verses 34b. Therefore, we realize that the content of the heart is words. This means the mouth speaks forth the content of the heart. Whatever the heart nurtures good or evil the mouth is only responsible to speak forth.

'Keep your heart with all diligence; for out of it are the issues of life' Proverbs 4 verses 23. Did you just read and hear what that scripture declares? Is there any meaning it has made in your heart? This is the word of God giving us the responsibility to seriously and carefully guide whatever information comes to our heart for out of it comes what affects our life matters and affairs. You should decide from this very moment what you will want to hear and what you will not want to hear, since it will affect your entire life and nobody will share the risk of the evil that happens but will want to take part of the good that happens in your life. Another very important question is what should I hear or allow into my heart? That is a very good question; I believe that your life has taken a new dimension today because you have decided to turn a new leaf as you direct the words in your mouth to bless as a fountain of blessing.

For that reason, alone I will show you what you need, to move to this next level you desire.

Now treasure within the context of this book refers to the Word of God, having the power and ability to cause all that affects your life flow in the direction that will turn you a Super victor in this life. This is further determined by what you believe and say concerning the kind of result, you crave.

The Heart is the House carrying your treasure (The Word of God). Do not let that thief (Satan) because of careless use of your words enter your house and steal your treasure, Mark chapter 4 verses 12, 14 and15. Therefore, it is applying the principle of the word that establishes the treasure you yearn for. With vision of the word at heart, you are able to map out the structures of your world, by knowledge garnishes the chambers with all precious and pleasant riches'. Proverbs 24 verses 3 and 4.

In this life, words determine our future. It does not matter whether someone believes it or not, because as the scriptures says out of the abundance of the heart the mouth speaketh. Looking at Genesis chapter one, we see that all that came into existence are the product of the word. God said, and God said, so on. What He said was manifest. Today it has not changed. We are made, in his image and likenesses, meaning to function in his capacity and given the legal right and privilege to create our world through the eye of His word in the gospel of His Christ. What a blessing!

Speak Life

Proverb chapter 18 verses 21 declares that 'life and death are in the power of the tongue and they that love it shall eat the fruit thereof'

Matthew 12 verses 37 declare 'For by the words thou shalt be justified, and by thy words thou shalt be condemned'.

'A man shall be satisfied with good by the fruit of his mouth': a proverb 12 verses 14, the amplified version says how forcible right words are.

Our world, family, relationship, today good or bad is affected and is the product of what we say. 'Even so the tongue is a little member, and boasteth great things, Behold, how great a matter a little fire kindleth. Moreover, the tongue is a fire, 'James chapter 3 verses 5 and 6b.

A man is a product of what he said yesterday, whether he is aware of the fact. The tongue utters words with a result positive or negative.

It really matters what you say about yourself and your future, because we were formed and fashioned by God to have our life go in the direction that we picture our lives to go using our mouth. God almighty did not give us the mouth to say foul things, nor curse or say how life circumstance and predicament has turned us weak, confused and wretched. Rather to create the kind of future we want to see and leave in. Therefore, what do you intend to turn positive in your life for the future you desire and picture? Your mouth can truly get you there; I mean that destination you desire to attain.

There was this story about a couple who for lack of knowing the principle of utterance, thought because they were both in love with each other could just express their love with words of death. The husband asked the wife if he dies what she will do, she replied that she was going to die too. It sound funny but that was very serious.

A few years later, the husband was travelling for an assignment and, of the entire occupant; he alone died in a car accident. The wife got the shocking news of what transpired, and could not believe her fortune. On her way to witness the fact about her husbands' death was involved in a car accident and died.

This couple misused their tongue, a wonderful treasure for building their destiny, to destroy themselves.

Every word you utter today is a stepping-stone to your destiny. I liken words to bricks. As you utter words whether good or evil, you lay foundations and in continuity build your destiny. Likewise, every brick you lay upon another gradually form the rooms of the house you are constructing. If you lay broken bricks, your house will definitely collapse. Speak life, no matter the circumstance you find yourself. Do not allow yourself be controlled by inordinate emotion not consistent with God's word for your life, rather be moved in your spirit through the word to initiate relevant change for a glorious future. Do not forget your words are treasures for piloting your future; guide it with all passion and jealousy.

The Seed Principle

'While the earth remains, seed time and harvest, cold and heat, summer and winter, and day and night shall not cease'. Genesis 8:22.

'Verily, Verily, I say unto you, except a corn of wheat fall into the ground and die, it abideth alone: but if it dies, it bringeth forth much fruit', John chapter 12 verses 24.

Seed is sown according to the level God has placed you, as the Spirit convicts. Nevertheless, the kind of seed am talking about here is the giving of your of your best or last cash. However, someone can still sow out of his abundance based on his need. The focal point here is one expecting the impossible in the physical realm as he sows his last and now looks up to God in faith to receive a miracle. The seed principle is not different from what we see the farmer does as in sowing seeds in the soil of his farm. Those seeds sown must die for the fruit of the seed to show up. We see, Jesus putting to practice the seed principle, as the only son of God dies for the sin of the world, that he might give birth too many sons in the kingdom. Today we are the fruit of redemption.

As a child of God you have to realize that it really matters what you do with your money, words, actions because they are seeds that will turn out your future a blessing or curse, not for you alone but for generations yet unborn. Paul the Apostle came to the realization of this truth so said, in Galatians chapter 6 verses 7 'Don't be misled-you cannot mock the justice of God. You will always harvest what you plant. Those who live only to satisfy their sinful nature will harvest decay and death from that sinful nature. But those who live to please the Spirit will harvest everlasting life from the Spirit'.

Sowing for a just course

Make up your mind and plan to sow for a just course. Collaborate with God and invest for kingdom business. You are privilege, to encounter a truth like this. There are many out there, who just need to hear a word of hope to get back on their feet. You can make a difference in their lives by sowing for the purchase of, 'FULFILLING YOUR GOD GIVEN DESTINY', and have it sent to them. 'Then he said unto them, Go your way, eat the fat, and drink the sweet, and send portions unto them for whom nothing is prepared: neither be ye sorry; for the joy of the Lord is your strength', Nehemiah 8 verse 10.

There are those who nothing have been prepared for and God is looking up to you and saying 'son/daughter you can make a difference with that seed money in your hands. If you can let that money go I will take care of your generation unborn, if you let that for kingdom investment I will transport you to your next level, if you can say yes Lord to me I will change your business and enlarge your coast'. What people need in our world today that decays in wickedness and evil, is redemptive knowledge, and that is what this book has brought through the inspiration of the Spirit?

The seed in your hands is your treasure, and the giver is the house that conveys the seed. It is important you understand that whatever you give for the propagation of the gospel of Christ secures your destiny in God and your generation. The seed connects you to kingdom establishment and blessings. Let me share with you, what seed power can do for anyone.

A servant of God, whose son lost his mind, was brought to a medical practitioner who seeing the condition of the boy knew that there is nothing as a medical practitioner he could do about the young boy's health, as it was beyond the scope of the medical world. He told the father of this boy to have the child dumped in a medical institution and forget that he ever had a son. Instead this man of God, took this boy back home, looking straight into the mothers face with the expression of faith on his face, said to his wife 'we going to have a miracle'. Further saying that they were going to give to God what they have never given before. She asked, in desperation 'what do we have to give?' He answered we are giving to God $200,000. But we are only having $2000, she said. Guess what, this couple took all they had and sold them and were able to realize the money. In tears [He that goeth forth and weepeth, bearing precious seed, shall doubtless come again with rejoicing, bearing his sheaves with him psalm 126 verses 6] and faith, along with his child, he went to his church and placed the money on the altar.

At that moment it came to pass the long desired and awaited miracle took place, the child's health restored by the power of God. What a miracle!

Today, this child does what any normal child does and is an excellent student.

The future of that child was right in the father's seed, what would have then, been the fate of this child if the father failed to sow that seed? Thank God the father did so, and sowed the saving seed. Your seed power is your saving power. You can make a difference right now, is just a step of faith in His word and the story is changed.

The church Principle

'And so, dear brothers and sisters, I plead with you to give your bodies to God because of all He has done for you. Let them be living sacrifice-the kind He I will find acceptable. This is truly the way to worship him'. Romans chapter 12 verses 1, NLT.

God is interested in you more than anything you could think or offer in this life. He wants to build His house in you. Jesus said when a man believes in Him; with the Father will make their home in that man. He has put eternity in the heart of man, that his plans and purposes be fulfilled through man on earth. You are God's focus and attention. This idea is the greatest of all in this book. The kingdom of God, cannot be detected by visible signs. Luke chapter 17 verse 21 you will not be able to say, 'Here it is! On the other hand, 'it's over there!' For the kingdom of God is already among you [within you, meaning in your heart]. Luke 17 verses 20 and 21.

Jesus Christ made it possible through his death and resurrection to have God living in everyman for kingdom exploit. Therefore, you realize that destiny is fulfilled as you work in God's grand purpose of the kingdom, and which is to affect the world of sinners and edify the saints in the body of Christ. You were manifested to make an impact, to shine as the light in this dark world. Your light is important as to light up lives of men and women who have been doomed in the darkness of evil. There are many out there, you desire to reach out the hand of help to, however, you cannot do it as a person, except through the gospel message.

You can only give your loved one, neighbour, friends hope and faith with the message of the gospel. It is only the message of the gospel that has the power to reach and meet every need of man no matter the severity. Giving copies of this book to people you really love will do things beyond your wildest imaginations. I have touched many lives with books of many Christian authors. They say things that touch my heart, which has made me a super believer today; I give glory and thanks to God, for the privilege of making me a blessing to someone.

No great joy in this life like affecting lives for kingdom purpose, that people turn at you with a smile and say God bless you for being a blessing to me.

Self Denial

'He that taketh not his cross, and followeth me, is not worthy of me. He that findeth his life shall lose it: and he that loseth his life for my sake shall find it.' Matthew 10 verses 38 and 39.

It is true that one has to be a fool to be a disciple of Jesus Christ. Being a fool here means acting in accordance or in complete compliance with the knowledge of the scriptures consistent with the gospel of Jesus Christ. In order words crucifying your will power, personal decision, whatever you like to enjoy as a human being. You decide to lose interest and desire to worldly pleasures, and take upon yourself to live and fulfil the will of Christ on earth. I remember spending most of my time with a young chap who always wanted to prove a point, how he always wanted to show in everything that so and so was wrong and he was right. If you always look at things within your perspective, you will never see a good from anybody you have dealings. Proverb chapter 14 verses 12 say, 'there is a way that seems right unto a man but the end thereof is destruction'.

This was the same with the Pharisee in the days of Jesus. Because they had some knowledge of the law, they saw Jesus to be the devil that tuned the heart of many to himself. We saw Jesus doing the good they could not do in there very presence and community.

Do you realize that it came to the point that a man called Jesus, good master? Jesus replied 'there is no good but God the Father in heaven'. Jesus only wanted his credit from the heavenly Father, never from his own mouth did he justify himself, even though he was right to have justified himself. He had his will and way to live the kind of life he desired for himself but choose to fulfil the will of [The Father]. He denied himself from all the pleasure in the heaven lies, to a low life amongst mere men, trampled by his own beloved brethren. Who in the world of men can stand that?

To present ourselves to God as a living sacrifice means denial of Self-gratification for God-glorification. When you present yourself to God, you are actually telling Him to take His property and mould it to his desire and taste. As soon as he gains access to your body, he connects your destiny in him prepared from the foundation of the world. Never think twice when presenting your body as a living sacrifice to God, He is not a man and will not fail you. This, you do, in a heartfelt prayer.

CHAPTER FIVE

THE TRADITION OF THE SPIRIT

'If we live by the [Holy Spirit] Spirit, let us also walk by the Spirit. (If by the Holy Spirit we have our life in God, let us go forward walking in him, our conduct controlled by the Spirit)'. Galatians chapter 5 verses 25 AMP

'But I say, walk and live [habitually] in the Holy Spirit responsive to and controlled and guided by the Spirit then you will certainly not gratify the cravings and desire of the flesh (of the human nature without God'. Galatians chapter 5 verses 16 AMP

"Therefore, brethren stand fast, and hold the traditions which ye have been taught, whether by word, or our epistle."2thessalonians chapter 2 verses 15 KJV.

There is such a thing as the tradition of the Spirit. What does this denote? That the moment one is born again and Spirit filled, he has been born into a family that has traditions and the Holy Spirit is the originator of such traditions, meant to build the character of kingdom citizens.

Tradition is custom and practice from the past passed on as accepted standard of behaviour for the present. Every tribe on earth has a tradition, a product of the five senses. These traditions are formed from what we see, hear, smell, feel and taste. The natural man responds to these traditions administered by the five senses, because it is within his circle of moral existence. This tradition becomes his code of conduct, to trespass these traditions will mean doing injustice to the law of the land as established. The natural man is bound within his community to leave in complete yields to these traditions as life guiding principles.

The man that is regenerated has it different, because in him resides the new creation life according to 2corinthians chapter 5 verses 17, 'Therefore if any person is (engrafted) in Christ (the messiah) he is a new creature (a new creature altogether), the old (previous moral and spiritual condition) has passed away, behold, the fresh and new come!' The believer in Christ is to conduct himself in accordance to the new personality in Him (Christ), through the power of the Spirit.

The new creation doesn't and must not live according to the previous moral and spiritual condition. This is so, because his old personality died with Christ on the cross. He now walks and lives his life in accordance with the tradition of the Spirit not in accordance with the tradition of the natural man.

The natural man is ruled and governed by the traditions (life guiding principle) from the sense realm, while the spiritual man in Christ is governed by the tradition of the Spirit (life guiding principles). Knowledge destroys ignorance and the truth free one from the darkness of evil. Knowledge is the fuel to fulfilling your God given destiny.

The reason many Christians are unable to be result oriented in every facet of their life, is that, most have been too used to the sense realm, having the sense realm dominant in their mindset and function with sensual principles for spiritual application. Unknown to him he becomes stagnated from making substantial progress in life. To walk in the Spirit is to make a practice of the spiritual traditions (principles), till a Godly mindset is produced in your pattern of thinking and behavior.

As a believer, you must learn to be patient with God in his dealings in our personal lives. Most believers are in haste to attain maturity, and that is why at certain point of growth in their lives tending to exercise certain spiritual virtue not yet attained. That is where there is missing link. They begin to feel and think that, God reciprocate their feeling and thinking in that particular level or point they claim to operate, unknown to them that the flesh was speaking. Understand that you have no rival in Christianity to rub shoulders with, to prove a point that you have attained. Your past is your rival. So take your time to learn the tradition of the family where you hail, to understand better how to go about things.

The dispensation of the Spirit is today, with the New Testament believer, His power is at work in the church of Jesus Christ, revealing to the church the person of Jesus Christ.

The Holy Spirit is what the Greek word call Allosparakletus, meaning one called alongside to help or one of the same kind. His ministry in our lives as believers is indispensable; receiving His ministry is absorbing His nature and spirit in our human spirit. In order words, you imbibe His tradition into your human spirit as you yield to his voice. We receive our life from the Holy Spirit in God and we must endorse His guiding light in our human spirit to fulfill our destiny in God.

The principle of the Spirit

The Holy Spirit dwell in the heart of Christians whom He has renewed and sanctified, to guide and assist them in their duties. He is that gracious principle who manifests His characteristics in the souls and spirits of His people, fighting against the principle of the flesh in them as the flesh fight against the Spirit. The Christian is to set himself under the guidance and influence of the blessed Spirit, and be agreeable to the motions and tendencies of the new nature in him.

'But I say walk and live habitually in the Holy Spirit responsive to and controlled and guided by the Spirit, then you will certainly not gratify the cravings or desires of the flesh of human nature without God', Galatians chapter 5 verses 16. AMP.

The tradition of the Spirit is the unveiled or revealed knowledge of God's word, implanted in the believer to build his habit to respond to, and be controlled and guided by the Spirit as he contemplates the scriptures. In order words he is programmed only to respond to the Spirit life. The new creature, prosperity, communication, fellowship, relationship, life style, warfare, righteousness, knowledge, faith, is all in the Spirit as he contemplates the word, these virtues is exercised in his human spirit. The time is ripe that the believer walks away from shadows, and embrace the reality of the spiritual life, living in it tradition.

The word Governing Principle

'Therefore, brethren stand fast, and hold the traditions which ye have been taught whether by word, or our epistle'2 Thessalonians chapter 2 verses 15.

The word of God is that principle, communicated and practiced in the Spirit. It functions in the world of those who recognize and assimilate it creative power, foreseeing the reproductive and creative power.

Paul was enlightening the Thessalonians believers to hold fast to the traditions and instructions of his mouth teachings and written epistles. The Thessalonians Believers were to allow their lives express his mouth teachings and hand written letters. Paul communicated to them that way because, he understood that there life and progress in the faith journey solemnly depend on his teachings. If the believer is faced with challenge in his life, that could result to the fact that he does not know or the non-application of the word in daily undertakings. Do not forget that you are the replica of God's word as the Spirit words perfect your destiny. Every Christian must come to that understanding taking the word of God in the governance of every affair of their life.

John declares in the beginning (before all time) was the word (Christ) was with God from the beginning. All things were made and came into existence through Him, and without Him was not even one thing made that has come into being. In Him was life, and the life was the light of men. John chapter 1 verses 1-4. AMP. He (in his love) chose us (actually picked us out for Himself as His own) in Christ before the foundation of the world, that we should be holy (consecrated and set apart for him) blameless in His sight, even above reproach, before Him in love. These scriptures express our very origin before the very creation of the universe. He, GOD ALMIGHTY chose us in Christ before the foundation of the world for His purpose that we be blameless in love. That means the word had already decided our path and destiny in God. We were made to be in and under the government of God's word. We have been ordained to function within the prescribed limits of the Word of God. Outside the Word of God is no love, grace, mercy, faith and hope. The word of God governs and pilots our lives to that destination God the Father had ordained right in His Word. So you see, beloved in Christ we were fashioned to function only through the principle of the Word of God and attain the God kind of success.

Jesus Christ while on earth always manifests the glory of the Father as He delivered the oppressed from the crutch of the devil. By His good works of healing and miracles through the influence of His preaching and teachings made us see and understand that the answer to man's misery was the Word of God.

'And they went to Capernaum; and straightway on the Sabbath day he enters into the synagogue and taught. And they were astonished at his doctrine: for he taught them as one that had authority, and not as the scribes. And there was in their synagogue a man with an unclean spirit; and he cried out, Saying let us alone; what have we to do with thee, thou Jesus of Nazareth? Art thou come to destroy us? I know thee who thou art, the only one of God. And Jesus rebuked him, saying, Hold thy peace, and come out of him. And the unclean spirit had torn him, cried out with a loud voice, he came out of him.' Mark chapter 1 verses 21-26 KJV.

'And it came to pass afterward, that he went throughout every city and village, preaching and shewing the glad tidings of the kingdom of God: and his disciples were with him . . . 'Luke chapter 8 verse 1 KJV.

Jesus Christ is our perfect example, showing us that all human problems answered to the solution of God's word irrespective of the severity of the problem or the long life span of that problem. The believer's life hails from the very word of God. However, the believer is not the result of something arising from a consequence of something else; rather we came to being, as we believe in the living Christ who is the very word of God. So that, the same word (Christ), proceeds out into our human spirit making us the very same word. This truth is beyond the comprehension of the human mind, but that is the working of the Holy Spirit as we say yes to Him and let our human senses that seek evidence or some kind of physical proof dead; we are elevated into the realms of glory. Abiding in the teachings of the word is letting the word govern us in its principles of daily living and victory over the flesh, senses and the devil.

CHAPTER SIX

A VISION OF GOD

'Where there is no vision (no redemptive revelation of God) the people perish; But he who keeps the law (of God, which includes that of man) blessed (happy, fortunate, and enviable) is he'. Proverb chapter 28 verses 19.

Meditating on the creations of God with a heart to appreciate His goodness and greatness, places us in a position to see through His eye, how He, in His mighty power came about these mighty works of creation brought into existence.

Look at the moon, sun, stars, the beautiful cloud in the sky, oceans, how did this came to be?

John tells us that 'in the beginning was the word and word was with God and word was God. The same was in the beginning with God'. Give attention to verses 3, because it carries the message of this chapter. All things were made by him; and without him was not anything made that was made.

We now understand and can conveniently say that all creation is a product of God's word as explained by the gospel of John chapter 1 verses1-3. It is also important to know that as John received this revelation from the Spirit of truth [the Holy Spirit]; he was referring to a personality so he used the word HIM. If you further read down to verses 11 you will realize he referred to Jesus as the word that made existing creation. Definitely we have come to discover in the word that the galaxies came to be, through the word of God [the person of Jesus]. John again through the words of Jesus makes us understand how Jesus said in chapter 8 of John verses 42b . . . for I proceeded forth and came from God; neither came I of myself, but He sent me. This has given us a clue that Jesus the word of God was in God before creation was made manifest. Through the force of the word in God, God saw the vision of how He was going to display all creation in good order, as the picture came to maturity in the mind of God, He spoke them out in the power of the Spirit and all came to be.

God's principle has not changed, as gods the scriptures call us in John chapter 10 verses 34, through the transformative and creative force of the word we are to see and have the vision of God in light of the Gospel of His Christ in the propagation of gospel truth.

God gave the children of Israel a vision through Moses their leader, after the deliverance from the wicked crotch of pharaoh. God as the master visionary had the picture of the land of Canaan painted on their minds, being a land flowing with milk and honey. This gave the Israelite a mental direction as going to a definite place to enjoy and have that freedom they were denied in Egypt to worship God. As having a sense of direction were not aimless in their pursuit. Though we know that many fell, out of their disobedience to God's word, so died on the way to the promise land, but the point is, because of the vision directly from God piloting them to a particular destination, it gave them focus. In that mixed multitude we still had some who for holding fast to the vision of their destination made it to the promise land.

A man will never know what his life and ministry will give birth to unless he has vision of God. To have a vision is not just to wake up one morning and decide to put something on paper and say, God called me and gave me a vision to do so and so. To have a vision of God is a metamorphosis of the WORD in your human spirit, establishing the creative force in your spirit passed on to your mind with a big picture of what God has ordained to achieve from the foundation of the world through you. This means as you yield your spirit and soul to the LORDSHIP OF THE WORD OF GOD, with nothing to hold on to except the word, God through His grace and infinite mercy hands you a VISION in your human spirit as the answer to the cry of many in your world. You cannot possess this kind of VISION if you not extraordinarily PATIENT. Patience is one of those virtues that will determine your extent in the vision and your capacity. God given vision always attracts God's provision for kingdom investment and advancement. Vision holds you in, in the direction it has ordained for you to go through. Vision keeps you focused careful and watchful. Makes you wise and smart, redeeming the time.

It enables you go through life predicament that would have hindered your expansion turning you a success. Vision grants the ability to make wise decisions without consultations. With vision you are sustained on the route to your destination. Vision propels like a car engine and keeps you inspired at all times.

The Word declares Where there is no vision (no redemptive revelation of God) the people perish. In other words, where there is no redemptive insight of God the people are destroyed. In a clear term, where there is no unveiled knowledge of God's word to save, the people perish. So people will be guided into absolute darkness if there is a lack of God's guiding light [the word]. Note: the creative force of the Word pictures the vision in a man's spirit.

' . . . But he who keeps the law blessed is he'.

The law here refers to the word. It can be put; he who keeps the law blessed is he.

The Word and the vision are inseparable, because the word pictures the vision.

Prophet Amos in his day had a revelation of future scarcity of God's word and how important the word of God was to saint of his day. He likened the word of God to the physical food and water. We are in that day where the Word of God is scarce and people are really wondering about for solutions outside the word.

Moreover, without the redemptive revelation of the word, people perish or group in darkness. It follows that, the revealed truth about a problem through the word, is the means through which solution possible. Amos clearly tells us that people will wonder in darkness because there is no vision of the word to guide the people grouped in darkness.

'Behold, the days are coming, says the Lord God, when I will send famine in the land, not the famine of bread, nor a thirst for water, but a (a famine) for hearing of the word of the Lord. And (the people) shall wonder from sea to sea and from the north even to the west, they shall run to and fro to seek Word of the Lord (inquiring for and requiring it as one requires food), but shall not find it' Amos chapter 8 verses 11-12 AMP.

Amos here, in the phrase 'Word' likens it to physical food and water we consume in a daily bases. It is clear that when a man is restrained from eating and drinking, death follows next. Similarly, when God's word, which is life to the human spirit, is scarce according to Amos, the spirit will be dead. The individual's progress will gradually deteriorate, as he loses health and material resources.

Things are different when the word of God is abundant in vision form, a man easily finds his way through life, because through the word, understanding and knowledge are made available and that makes life have an established direction.

When people live in misery you just know that they are outside God's will for their lives. If a man runs to the north, east and west in search of the word without getting a solution to his darkness [problem], it means those places lack genuine servants of God. God's chosen servants are the custodian of the undiluted word of God. As the word is declared from their mouth it possesses the ability to inspire a change and proffer solution to the misery of man. When the word is scares as prophet Amos said, it means two different facts are the cause. One that, most people are blind to recognize real servants of God [as the god of this world has blinded their mind, lest the light of the glorious gospel should shine upon their heart, 1 Corinthians chapter 4 verses 3 and 3] or two that true and genuine servants of God are very few in number in a particular geographical location, to declare God's council.

The word of God is the guiding light we ever will need to direct our path in the centre of God's plan and purposes for our lives. As you vision the future, the word of God brings it to pass, sustaining and keeping you inspired till your vision is completely manifested amongst those you were called to minister to.

What can you see from where you are? It is what you see, that determines your placement in life.

The fuel of Vision

Vision is fuel to the spirit and mind. It is first down loaded to the human spirit and as the Spirit [The Holy Spirit] dominates the mind He makes possible the transfer of that vision to the mind realm. Vision is as fire, burning through a man's mind, which endows him with strength of heart to pursue without being obstructed. The vision of God makes him see life through the eye of his mind in the light of the Word. Vision motivates, inspires, and sustains the life of the visionary in the content and context of his vision propelling his heart like a lion panting after his sighted prey in a distant land.

The moment fuel exhaust in a car, we know the engine ceases to function and goes off. You see, it is not different from a man who ceases to take in to his human spirit a daily dose of the word, that vision will soon lose its flaming power. The word of God is the fuel of vision and vision is the fuel to the human spirit and mind. Vision causes urgency, fervent burning in your human spirit that keeps you refreshed and moving. A man with vision spares and spends no time for things that do not foster his vision. He meditates all day on possible means and ways the vision will break bounds and limitations and ensure the liberty of the defenceless, helpless and oppressed. Associates with people who are vision driven in like minds.

Vision swallows in victory whatever challenge arising in your life and ministry, it doesn't recognize the icon of detours. This is what vision will do in your human spirit; when you dwell in the Word of God and allow it through the confessions of your mouth as you say what God says, 'more than a conqueror, greater is he that lives in me than he that is in the world' and so on, I mean declare more scriptures as the Spirit brings to your remembrance or gives you utterance, it will create cloud of pictures of victory on your mind concerning your destiny in God. Vision holds the heart firm in the days of trouble.

Never be in a haste to get a vision, allow the word of God express himself, character, attribute, creative power and drive you through hardness and tough situations and show you how to overcome. As you exercise your human spirit in the assignment, the word of God gives you through the instruction of the Spirit and prospers in it. Then get ready for great things, as He will show you and take you to higher realms of glory on your mission in God.

The word has always shown and travelled in the power of the Spirit with people through revelation knowledge to have insight about His [the word] works of old during creation and with the prophets of old who in brokenness and passionate yield did great works in sacrifice to God almighty. This has not changed, the word wants to paint and picture your mind today as you study and meditate on the living word with grace, glory and power in the knowledge of Christ. And as you are fired up in His vision for the kingdom people's life have a new meaning to you. Remember, you must have the word to have vision.

The word empowers the vision

The creative force of the word is the determinant of the kind of vision you walk in to fulfilling your God given destiny, as the Word become the very dominant force that controls your life. See, you must yearn for;

desire to see the scriptures beyond written words. This is the work of the HOLY SPIRIT, but He only works with your desire, He will make your passionate desires to possess certain characteristics in the word so to you, as you study. To function in that kind of realm where you get the Father's attention in all that involves your personal life for the benefit of others in your world. You must live and think like an insane person to this world's system, and that must definitely mean there is something already controlling your whole thinking process being the word of the Spirit. When I say must act insane I mean what gives the world pleasure, doesn't give you pleasure. Then make a deliberate effort to respond with action whenever the Holy Spirit demands you to perform immediately an assignment. As you pant after the word to understand deeper truths, you begin to receive information from the Spirit in pictures. This is a realm that has an instilling experience, where you really come to better appreciate the goodness of God for making, us share in His glory through His son.

'Where there is no vision the people perish;' the scriptures says the people group in darkness, meaning they are ignorant of reality. Vision is life, because vision gives reason purpose and plan for existence. Vision is a child of the word of God, this means the life of vision hails from the word. Did Jesus have a vision? Yes, Jesus did have a vision. His vision was making men/women kingdom citizens, as they repented (change their heart from evil to good). He taught them that doing the will of God the Father, which was doing His word, was the key to a successful and great life in God. The more Jesus taught the word about the kingdom and met needs, faith, hope and love was stirred in their heart, having their focus sustained and maintain in the hoped kingdom.

'Another parable spake he unto them; 'The kingdom of heaven is like unto leaven, which a woman took, and hid in three measures of meal, till the whole was leavened'. Verses 36, Then Jesus sent the multitude away, and went into the house: and his disciples came unto him, saying, declare unto us the parable of the tares of the field. He answered and said unto them, He that soweth the good seed is the Son of man; the field is the world; the good seed are the children of the kingdom; but the tares are the children of the wicked one; The enemy that sowed them is the devil; the harvest is the end of the world; and the reapers are the angels.' Matthew chapter 13 verses 33,36-39.

The parable Jesus taught about the kingdom was the word that sustained the heart of his disciples keeping them on track or path of the kingdom.

In life, we must always have a committed direction to our destination and must be inspired with vital information until we get to our destination. We witnessed this practiced by Jesus, as he shared vital truths necessary to prosper his disciples to the kingdom. If the sick man/woman will only have vision of God regardless of the severity of the sickness and declare faith in God's word, they will stand up strong and healthy. Dexter Yeager was facing some challenge with his health, unable to move his body. He had a vision of God, spoke to himself about his future, and refused to be held back by sickness as he stood up by faith walking into strength and health.

I understand the feeling of pain in the body can bring such a discomfort, which may stagger for faith in the word for healing. However, you can prevail holding yourself in, through understanding. Understand that the enemy inflict sever pain so that the sick or diseased will lose the sight of faith in the word tending to see impossibility. Nevertheless, as you hold in by faith in the word, and believe that of a truth, Jesus healed many sick and faith in him will bring health into your body, deciding to serve him with your life. I tell you the truth without an iota of doubt you will have a miracle.

With vision, you can get your finance, health, business and project back. See their restoration through eye of vision and nothing will by any means resist you.

At age 28 Watchman Nee was facing a severe cough and later was revealed by a man called Dr. Wong that he had tuberculosis. After he was X-rayed the doctor said, to him 'you should not come to me anymore I would only be stealing your money. There is no hope for you'. Watchman Nee made a statement to the Lord; here is what he said, 'Lord, how can this be happening'? He asked, 'I have so many things to do for you. How can the end come when I've only begin'?

The victory scriptures that got him back on his feet was 2 Corinthians chapter 1 verses 24, 'by faith you stand', 'we walk by faith' 2 Corinthians 5 verses 7, 'and all things are possible to him who believes'.

He slowly rose from his deathbed and dresses himself in cloths he had not worn for a hundred and seventy-six days. He remembered those words, 'Walk by faith'.

He took two steps and started to faint. Where do you want me to go he asked the Lord? The answer came: Go downstairs to Sister Lee's room, with each step he cried out, 'Walk by faith, walk by faith!' With the twenty-fifth and final step, he got his healing.

Do you now understand how the word empowered the vision in the heart of Watchman Nee.

That is the same confessional pattern in the word you exercise to be restored in any part of your life troubled by the enemy of your soul. The answer to whatever desire of your heart is in your vision. Yes, the word has been sent into your human spirit to strengthen that vision in your heart. Hallelujah!

CHAPTER SEVEN

GIVING A KEY

'For God so loved the world that he gave his only begotten son, that whosoever believeth in him should not perish, but have everlasting life'. John chapter 6 verses 38. KJV

'Give, and it shall be given unto you; good measure, pressed down, and shaken together, and running over, shall men give into your bosom. For with the same measure that ye mete withal it shall be measured to you again'.

'Give to every man that asked of thee . . .' Luke chapter 6 verses 30.

Many have aired their views on the subject of giving, in the application of human sense, in the avoidance of money monger ministers, who they say centre their messages on money giving, as a prerequisite for financial prosperity.

This has caused internal financial challenge amongst some local churches in the body of Christ that has affected belief of individual believers who have decided to take this as an issue of importance to themselves. The devil has also traded on the ignorance of the believers regards this issue of giving, to rob the church of greater blessings in spiritual realms.

When it comes to the subject of giving, the scriptures have laid down principles on how we are to give. We will consider those principles one after the other.

The word of God is always ready with answers and solution to whatever challenge in life is it we face. If we on our part will sincerely desire the word to have final say on issues that has become a torn on the flesh, then we will leave in victory.

From the first scriptures above, John tells us God gave His only Son, He had for the benefit of the entire humanity. We see in the scriptures that the devil never gave; instead, the scripture recognizes the devil as a thief.

This means that giving is the attribute of God almighty.

Primarily what stirs up the act of giving? Of course, need stirs up giving.

The needs here are in two faces, the need of the giver and the need of the receiver.

Giving to all men

'Give to anyone who ask, and when things are taken away from you, don't try to get them back.' Luke chapter 6 verses 30. If it was true that you made Jesus your LORD, and then this is what he is saying to you, give to anyone who asks. Give what you have as you are asked, it's impossible to take away from a Christian, because all things are his. A Christian is a spirit being and the scriptures have made legal to him both spiritual and physical resources, which makes all he own spiritually protected. The master knew this so he said, do not struggle with he that forcefully desires to have to himself what belongs to you, he is only shadow boxing'.

The spiritual and the physical world are under the control of the believer in Christ. Using your sense to determine, what you are to do about your giving life style, because of some folks who for their wrong mindset in making money out of people's pocket, for their personal pleasure is foolishness according to the scriptures, 'The way of a fool is right in his own eyes: but he that hearkeneth to council is wise' proverbs chapter 12 verses 15.

You are a blessing to humanity, is important you know this fact.

Humanity must feel your impact in this world, no two ways about that because you were fashioned to make an impact. Now that God has helped you achieve some level of success, the responsibility is on you to touch lives of people in your world. You do not have an excuse for not affecting others. In John chapter 3 verses 16, reads for God so love people in the world, that He gave his only begotten son . . .' God Loved people and gave them a lively hope, it is expected of us as his children to express that godly attribute we have seen Him manifest.

God saw the vision of the entire human race and through the sacrificial offering of His son touched all who believe. God still loves all men and rest His blessings upon them even today. Do the same.

The way of a fool is right in his own eyes: but he that hearkeneth unto counsel is wise.' Proverbs 12 verses 15.

Giving to the body of Christ

'As we have therefore opportunity, let us do good unto all men, especially unto them who are of the household of faith.' Galatians chapter 6 verses 10.

The scripture recognizes doing good to all men when we have the opportunity to demonstrate generosity. Then it says exceptionally to the believer in Christ. This means God wants us to do good to the believer in Christ because we belong to one family in Christ. There are believers that are poor amongst us, that a little push of help will place them strong on their feet. What have you done about that poor saint living in your neighbourhood?

Giving to servants of God

'He that receiveth a prophet in the name of a prophet shall receive a prophet's reward; and he that receiveth a righteous man in the name of a righteous man shall receive a righteous man's reward.' Matthew 10 verses 41.

Surely, the Lord God will do nothing, but he revealeth his secret unto his servants the prophets. Amos chapter 3 verses 7.

' . . . Believe in the Lord your God, so shall ye be established; believe his prophets, so shall ye prosper.'2 chronicles chapter 20 verses 20b God has placed prosperity in the hands of his servants the prophet and it is only the key of giving that helps in contacting that prosperity. In the Old Testament you don't appear before a prophet empty handed, in demand for a blessing. We see this with Isaac how he told Esau his first some to go get him venison for a blessing. If you are a good Bible student, you will know that his younger brother Jacob out smart him through the advice of his mother Rebecca. However, the point here is this; it was that venison that got Jacob the blessing.

'And he said unto him, Behold now, there is in this city a man of God, and he is an honourable man; all that he saith cometh surely to pass: now let us go thither; peradventure he can shew us our way that we should go.

Then said Saul to his servant, but, behold, if we go, what shall we bring the man? For the bread is spent in our vessels, and there is not a present to bring to the man of God: what have we? And the servant answered Saul again, and said, Behold, I have here at hand the fourth part of a shekel of silver: that will I give to the man of God, to tell us our way'. 1 Samuel chapter 9 verses 6 to 8.

If you really want to make enviable progress and impact in God's kingdom, then you must learn to act wise in the word.

Look at the shunem woman in 1 king's chapter 4 verses 8-17. The woman knew and understood how to contact God's anointing in His servant. She made a chamber for Prophet Elisha to lie in, and provided him with meal. Elisha was moved with this woman's smart goodness and the anointing to meet her need began to function on Elijah. He sent Gehazi his servant to call her. As she appeared before Elijah, he spoke through Gehazi in request of her desire. 'Should I talk to the King or the captain to give you your heart desire?' he asked. If that woman desired her enemies destroyed, that would have happened. This is the anointing it can do anything. God honours the words of His servants to perform their decrees. Gahazi Elijah's servant immediately answered for the woman telling Elijah she had no child. Elijah called her as she came close to him, He uttered anointed words, I mean words clothed with divine potency. About this season, according to the time of life, thou shall embrace a son . . .' 2kings 4verses 16. The word of God's servant came to pass in verses 17, and the woman conceived and bore a son at the season that Elijah had said unto her according to the time of life. Life becomes full of glory and beauty the moment the anointing from the servant of the most high is at work.

Be wise and smart enough to know that you can change the circumstance of your life when you walk in accordance with the words of God's servant.

Giving for the gospel

The Gospel of Jesus Christ simply put, means good news. Good news to the sick, you are healed by his stripes, 1peter chapter 2 verses 24, himself bore our sins in his body on the tree, that we, being dead to sin, should live unto righteousness: by whose tripe's ye were healed. Good news to the poor, he becomes poor so that you might be rich, 2corithians chapter 8 verses 9.

Good news to the sinner, he has given you a nature superior to sin nature and that of the devil, Matthew 9 verses 13 . . . for I am not come to call the righteous, but sinners to repentance. For the gospel to get to the ends of the earth, it takes mega bulks. Jesus issued the command to preach the gospel to all nations of the earth. You have no option but to do as he said, knowing that He is the master. You must send forth missionaries or find yourself in the mission field.

The good news is indispensable as it is the power of God unto salvation, Roman 1 verses 16. God can't heal, prosper and deliver a man outside the gospel, because He has placed his power in the gospel, Romans 1 verses 16. Your dollars, pounds, euro will get this gospel job done. Believe it and give it. Beyond your imagination, God will put a new song in your mouth

CONCLUSIONS

The answer to all life challenge is in hands of those men and women who God has chosen to reveal His secret.

Prophet Amos said, 'surely the Lord will do nothing but He reveals His secret to his servants the prophet'. God is still speaking these last days to His servants all over the entire world.

God is speaking through preaching, teaching, tape and in the book, Fulfilling Your God Given Destiny.

Fulfilling your God Given Destiny is that secret of God unveiled through God's servant revealed to you, to inspire and direct your path in God. This book as you passionately and meditatively yield your mind and spirit to this truth, will find and walk in that path God has orchestrated for you from the foundations of the world.

Finally, as you open your mind to assimilate the realities in this book, God's Spirit will turn you another man. You are more than a conqueror through Him that called you. Amen.

ABOUT THE AUTHOR

Prince E A Jeshurun is a Humanitarian worker, teacher of the word, an author. He resides presently in Nigeria. He is the author of the governing principle in the real world. The author is an expository and social conscience writer and passionate about bringing clarity into issues and subject of doubt in the body of Christ, who also believes that the believer will better enjoy and express his liberty in Christ in his world, when his social contacts are influenced with principled living.

He has a higher diploma in Public Administration, diploma in public relations from the Royal Society Academy, Ibadan Nigeria, and a diploma in computer application.

An Insight of the Book

This book pictures reasons for the unfulfilled life of Christians and ministers in the body of Christ, as some ministers lay hold on teaching in old testament laws and man made doctrines as a prerequisite for acceptance by God as grace. He unravels through the revelation of the

Spirit through the Word of God, anecdotes and illustrations how the unbeliever, believer and minister can fulfil their God Given Destiny.

It is a beautiful recipe for bible school, teaching programmes and inspirational guide for bible student into understanding maturity in Christ.